T0128379

One
Step
Forward

Michael J. Ewens

WESTBOW PRESS®
A DIVISION OF THOMAS NELSON
& ZONDERVAN

This book is a work of non-fiction. Unless otherwise noted, the author and the publisher make no explicit guarantees as to the accuracy of the information contained in this book and in some cases, names of people and places have been altered to protect their privacy.

WestBow Press books may be ordered through booksellers or by contacting:

WestBow Press
A Division of Thomas Nelson & Zondervan
1663 Liberty Drive
Bloomington, IN 47403
www.westbowpress.com
1 (866) 928-1240

Because of the dynamic nature of the Internet, any web addresses or links contained in this book may have changed since publication and may no longer be valid. The views expressed in this work are solely those of the author and do not necessarily reflect the views of the publisher, and the publisher hereby disclaims any responsibility for them.

Any people depicted in stock imagery provided by Getty Images are models, and such images are being used for illustrative purposes only. Certain stock imagery © Getty Images.

ISBN: 978-1-9736-7785-7 (sc)
ISBN: 978-1-9736-7787-1 (hc)
ISBN: 978-1-9736-7786-4 (e)

Library of Congress Control Number: 2019916665

Print information available on the last page.

WestBow Press rev. date: 10/18/2019

PROLOGUE

My story begins here, though my life began a long time ago. I did not know that, however, until April 2009. At the time, I was 48 years old. Until then, I always believed in God and knew that He intervened in our lives on a regular basis. Yet, I never gave Him full credit, in spite of the many occasions in my life, when I knew He was present.

Suddenly, my whole life and the world became clear to me, through His eyes. It wasn't the "near death" experience many have read about, nor was it sudden and miraculous, yet the culmination of a series of events, circumstances, and spiritual awakenings. After resisting for years, I gave up and my new life began.

chapter one:

The Early Years

I was born and raised Roman Catholic. It was 1959 and the Church was burgeoning with all their members, schools and missions. Among my immediate family (relatives, that is), we had one Catholic priest, along with 3 nuns. So, Church and religion was a big thing!

My mom considered entering the convent, but instead chose to have eight children. That's what happened back then – lots of big families. Dad was at work, and Mom was home with the kids.

Fortunately, with all the religion and prayers, we were always safe. Or so we thought?

My brothers and sisters attended the same Catholic elementary school and 2 of my brothers attended a Catholic High School. We had nuns teaching us in the classroom and the priests visiting and saying Mass. The nuns used discipline as their weapon and the nuns and priests used guilt to keep us in line.

I remember one nun in second grade, pulling the pigtails of a girl classmate, when she wasn't listening. I remember another scolding a male classmate because he batted his eyes. I saw several classmates getting their knuckles whacked by a long pointer. Fortunately for me, the worst penalty I received was placing gum on my nose until the end of class.

Aside from these examples of rewarded

behavior (just kidding here), there were so many rules, it was hard to keep track. For example, you could not receive communion, unless it had been at least an hour, since you had last eaten. If you didn't go to confession enough or attend Church, you were a sinner and you were going to hell.

That was the law of the day and that was what I and many others learned, as we tried to make our way through our youth and adolescence. Of course, the priests could not marry and males ruled the Church. We all know how that worked out over the years. Through all this, I wondered if there was something missing.

I do not recall any major circumstances, nor feelings throughout my childhood, when I felt the presence of the Holy Spirit, Jesus, or God. Of course, we were told the Trinity was alive in all of us and if we listen and pray, you will receive salvation. But how does an eight or twelve year old understand that and what sense does it make, when you hear the same stories, week in and week out?

All I recall is that I, (like my children at a similar age) was bored and could not wait for Church to be over, so I could play with my friends, watch television, or just hang out. In fact, by the time I was about 15, I managed to do just that, instead of attending church. By then, my parents had divorced and my mom had a tough time keeping track of all us kids.

Typically, my mom would go to church with a couple of the younger kids and I would plan to attend a later mass. I would show up at church, but then meet a friend outside, sneak to the grade school near the church, smoke cigarettes and then return home at the obligatory time.

Of course, we made sure to return to hear the Gospel from the back of the church, so we could prove we attended service. That was long enough and the plan worked well for many months and years. I always made sure to grab a Church bulletin as well, just in case.

At some point (maybe 17 or 18 years old), I stopped attending Church on a regular basis and became one of those "ChrEaster" people. You know them. They are the ones that show up only on Christmas and Easter. For those who are Lutheran, Protestant, Jewish, Muslim, or other non-Catholics, I expect it was the same.

Typically, a large group would show up and occupy the extra rows, with all the extended family in town for the holidays. Everyone dressed "to the nines" and perfectly groomed for these events, so the rest of the congregation was sure to see the show. Of course, they were all gone by the next week and you wouldn't see them again until the next holiday.

Around this time, I began to have some serious doubts about the Catholic faith and religion as a whole. I questioned the need to attend services and remain "faithful", while all around me I witnessed regular church goers who attended on Sundays and then sinned all week. That was one of my father-in-laws favorite topics.

This pattern continued while I attended college, sought employment, entered relationships and began my adult life. I still attended Church when I was home with my family for the holidays. I actually accompanied a friend in college on an occasional basis, longing for a sense of feeling and understanding. Yet, nothing ever happened to convince me this was where I belonged.

After that, I entered relationships which I knew were not healthy. I moved in with a girl when I knew it wouldn't work. I made job choices, contrary to my intuition. I even married my first wife, after I had already sensed that it might not be a good idea (By the way, we were married in a non-denominational Church). At one point, I attempted a cross-country trip, when it made no sense.

During these periods, I had friends and family who suggested otherwise and advised at various times. I listened part of the time, but mostly did what I wanted to do. I was selfish, alone and focused on my self-destructive behaviors. Little did I know, how much easier my life could have been, had I listened to my conscience, the Holy Spirit and God.

chapter two:

God Leads the Way

Most of us have seen the Star Wars and the Harrison Ford - Raiders of the Lost Ark movies. The message of the "Force" is a simple one. Let go of your feelings, Luke was told. Trust the force Luke. Not until Luke learns this and adopts this as his way of life, does his life and mission become clear. The same message is prevalent in the Bible, with respect to following Jesus and God.

Likewise, not until Indiana Jones takes the first step on an invisible bridge in the third 'Raiders' movie, does he realize that trust and faith will show him the way. Just prior to that event, his father (Sean Connery) was shot by the Nazis, in an attempt to coerce Indiana to pass through a dangerous tunnel, as his first step to ultimately find the "Holy Grail" - in this case, Jesus' wine cup from the last Supper.

While Sean Connery is lying on the ground with a bullet wound and his friends and the bad guys wait in another part of the caves, Indiana must first get through the initial passageway. This involves booby traps, knives, etc. to block the way. As Indiana begins to enter, his father begins reciting, "A penitent man shall pass, a penitent man shall pass". In an earlier scene, the two had reviewed the several steps and words necessary, to help them succeed.

At this point, Indiana Jones remembers these words and realizes this phrase means that he needs to kneel and bow before God. He does this just in time, to avoid the fate of previous others, who did not perform this holy act.

Next, there are a series of stones with various letters, which must be addressed and travelled, to make it to the next stage. Indiana remembers talking to his dad about following the footsteps of God. He begins to step on the appropriate steps which spell Jehova, but then realizes in Hebrew, this begins with the letter "I". After almost falling to his doom, Indiana makes it through this stage.

After a few more steps, Indiana arrives at the edge of a cliff and must cross from one side, to another. But, there is no bridge! He has no idea how to get across. Meanwhile, the scene reverts to Sean Connery saying, "You must believe". Shortly thereafter, Indiana takes a breath, along with the first step, and a bridge becomes visible.

After crossing, he then sprinkles sand to show the bridge and the 'way'.

This story ends when the bad guy chooses the wrong cup and Indiana chooses Jesus' carpenter's cup and drinks water from the fountain, thus attaining eternal youth. He also pours the water on his father's bullet wound and the wound is healed. Everyone lives happily ever after.

This scene and faith plays out in many other movies, including the second Santa Clause, with Tim Allen. At one point long after Tim becomes Santa, he finds out there is actually a 'Santa Clause', which requires that he marry, or he will no longer be Santa. He has little time to find a wife.

Fortunately, for Tim (or Santa), he meets his son's school principal and hopes to marry, though she does not believe his story. His son (a student at the school) shows his principal a snow globe which reveals the magic of Christmas and tells her that "Seeing isn't believing", but that, "Believing is seeing".

This is a test put forth in the Bible on many occasions, with regards to believing without seeing, as a testament to faith in God and Jesus.

A similar scenario plays out in the children's classic movie, Nemo. For those who have not seen the movie, Dory and Marlin are two fish in search of Marlin's son, Nemo, who is lost far away in the ocean. They encounter many struggles and obstacles along the way, as do we in our lives and on our path to God.

At one point, the two have been swallowed by a whale and are in the whale's esophageous area, holding on, so as not to get swallowed up in the belly. The whale moans something, which Dory attempts to interpret. She then instructs Marlin, "You need to let go".

Marlin is a bit of a worrier. He resists and asks Dory, "How do you know nothing bad is gonna happen?" Dory tells him, "I don't." She continues to urge Marlin to "let go". He finally does and of course, is exhilarated when they escape through the blow hole and are free to continue their journey to find Nemo.

The point is, you must put your faith in the Lord, especially when you are uncertain what will occur. This is the way, as told through Jesus' life. In the Bible and his teachings, over and over again, we are told to let go of earthly treasures, trust in His ways and see your life (and path to Heaven) become clear.

chapter three:

The Soul's Journey

Dozens of books have been written about the journey of the soul and its' link to conscious behavior and choices. When I think back on all the decisions I made, in direct contrast to my "gut feeling", I realize how my life could have been different.

Now, don't get me wrong here, because many of you will say those choices made me a "better person". Also, we can learn from our bad choices and use those lessons throughout our lives.

However, the question is whether we are free to make these choices, or is it left to chance or fate?

In the classic Clint Eastwood movie, 'A Mule for Sister Sarah', Shirley MacLaine plays a Catholic nun, who is escorted across hostile territory by Clint Eastwood in the United States during the French-Mexican conflict. He plays the role of a lone rugged cowboy (desperado), looking for treasure.

By circumstance, the two come together.

At one point, a deal is brokered, which allows Shirley MacLaine to lead Clint to the treasure, so long as he provides her protection against the French army. Aside from the entertaining and humorous action, there is a scene where Shirley asks Clint if he believes in God or miracles. He says no, and raises the question I have posed above (chance versus fate).

Clint tells the story of 2 men riding side by side. A bullet ricochets off a rock and kills one of them and does not kill the other. Clint said this is just an accident and not a miracle. He reasons there is no God, nor fate, but rather occurrences that happen by chance. In other words, the man was in the wrong place at the wrong time. Now, this may be the case, but is it really that simple?

God made man in his own image and provided us the opportunity for, "free will". That is a common understanding among many religions and is taught as a means to provide guidance. What does this mean though? Can we do whatever we want and not worry about the consequences, since this is our "destiny"?

Sure, you can do that, but more often than not, those choices will lead you to the same place each time. The alcoholic who continues to drink, will continue to be an alchoholic. The sex addict who continues the behavior, will continue to leave victims in his wake. The person who continues to make the wrong choices, will never be saved. We have all been there, or know many who have travelled this path. The end result is the same.

chapter four:

Choose Wisely

Throughout our lives, we are provided with opportunities to make choices, right or wrong. Depending on those choices, we set our path and determine our own destiny. God is present at all times, hoping you make the right choice. However, if you don't, God is still with you and will continue to provide opportunities, until you make the right choices and give your life to Him.

With reference to the scene mentioned above in the Indiana Jones movie, there is more to the story. At this point, the good guys and bad guys are now in a room. It is like a treasure room, with many gold goblets, including the aforementioned wine cup used by Jesus at the last supper. The belief is, that if you drink from the water well with this cup, you will have eternal youth.

In this room, there is a knight from the Christian Crusades, who is the last of 3 brothers, who swore to protect the room and the goblet for centuries. As soon as Indiana reaches the room, the Nazis follow and the leader chooses a cup, which he feels is that of Jesus. After he drinks from it, he is immediately turned to ashes, followed by a comment from the Knight, who says, "He chose poorly".

Next, Indiana Jones chooses a cup, which he feels is the right choice. Of course, he now has acquired some insight (and faith?), as he settles on a less glamorous and dirty cup (which appears to

correlate more with Jesus' common man status).
Indiana drinks and is told by the Knight, "You have
chosen wisely". He returns to Sean Connery, who
drinks from the cup and now lives.

With regards to choices and that cross country
trip I made years ago, I sensed I should not
attempt the trip, but went ahead with plans. I was
alone and driving from Los Angeles to Chicago, at
the end of December, to retrieve some belongings
I had left behind. I was in New Mexico and it began
snowing. The roads were becoming dangerous,
with a snow/ice mixture.

I was preparing to get off the freeway at
the next exit, when my truck slid on black ice. I
went off the road, flipped over three times and
landed (miraculously) on all four wheels in a ditch.
Needless to say, I was shell shocked and scared,

but did what I had to do, to get out of the ditch, find help and get on my way.

Had I listened to my intuition (my conscience, my soul, my God), I would not have begun that trip in the first place. In addition, I would not have the lifelong chronic back and neck pain, which resulted from this accident. Each day, I am reminded of this event, as I manage my care through exercise, massage therapy, chiropractic treatment and prayer. I made a clear choice and this is the result.

However, while I did not make the right choice, God has taken care of me throughout the years, relative to this pain. While I know and have witnessed many others with less pain, who have given up, I have been able to live a relatively normal life. However, this has not been without setbacks.

I recall a trip with my wife Ellen, many years ago. We were driving in the car. I was the passenger at the time. I have always used different positions, along with analgesic creams and patches, to alleviate my symptoms, in particular while driving. On this day, however, the pain was excruciating. All I could do was pray silently and ask God to somehow help me deal with the pain.

In an instant, I felt the presence of God and my actual father (who had passed not long before) and the pain dissipated. I immediately told my wife and a complete sense of warmth and freedom was prevalent. I made it home fine and returned to my daily activities.

chapter five:

Acceptance

Some of you may not believe this event occurred and at the same time ask, "What about events that occur that have nothing to do with a choice you made, yet send you and/or your family into a downward spiral?" This could be a random shooting which kills innocent people, a tragic accident, loss of a child, or genocide which we see in so many countries.

My wife and I had such an experience, when our full term second daughter Payton, was infected with Group B Strep. She lived on life support for two days and then was delivered safely to the Lord, when we discovered she had no brain activity. This occurred not because of a choice we made, but rather a random event, which turned our lives upside down.

At the time, we had a two year old daughter, Jayme, who was anxiously awaiting the birth of her little sister. She helped with all the preparations and had moved into her own "big girl" room, so that we could prepare the baby room for her sister. When we did not come home with the baby, she could not understand. How could such a thing happen?

This was a very difficult time in our lives and I have to say, a real strong test with our marriage. My wife and I handled it in different ways, through grief, support groups, prayer and crying sessions. The process took many, many months. At times, we just tried to make it through each day. We continued our attempts to have another baby, yet had miscarriages and no success.

At one point, we made a decision to adopt and completed all the planning, paperwork, and requisite courses, to first become certified foster parents. This qualified us as well in a fast track adoption program. We waited for our options to choose a child and one day, received a call about a 7 month old boy, looking for a home. We accepted him as a foster child and within 6 months, were able to complete a formal adoption.

His name (given by his birth mother) is Matthew, which means, "Child of God". He is now 15 years old and flourishing as a beautiful young man. Jayme missed her sister quite a bit the first several weeks and months, yet slowly accepted Matthew as her brother. This was difficult for her, since she made no decision to lose her sister and had to miss out on all their plans. We continue to miss Payton daily, but have grown as a family.

We have all heard that, "things happen for a reason". Try to explain that to a 2 year old girl and her parents, who have lost a sister and a child and the chance to watch her grow. Tell that to people who have lost their friends and family in struggles and wars worldwide. Convince victims of random crimes that, "God will show you the way".

It is a tough sell, but one we all have to face. Somehow, we have to make sense of it and look for a way to move on with our lives. I'm not sure Payton died for a reason, but I know that, had the tragic event not occurred, we would not have Matthew in our lives and perhaps, that was God's way?

Likewise, many of us have experienced or

witnessed the good that comes from tragic events or occurrences. How many times have people with "near death" experiences, turned that event into a life change, to help God's cause? How many times have we witnessed tragedies, which always seem to bring out the best in people, and lead to front page stories? Somehow, God's hand is at work.

chapter six:

Coincidences or not?

How many of you begin thinking about a particular person you had not heard from in a long time? For some reason, that person comes to mind and within a moment, you receive that phone call, text, or letter. How many of you have experienced a "feeling" or premonition that something will happen or has happened, and it turns out to be true?

These events have occurred in my life on many occasions. In my daily business as a vocational consultant, I work with many attorneys, though not always on a regular basis. Sometimes, I could go several weeks, without receiving a call or work from these attorneys. In other cases, it may be months or years.

In any case, many times a specific attorney will enter my mind, with whom I had not worked for a long time. Almost instantaneously, I will receive a call from that attorney. The same phenomenon occurs with a particular friend of mine, whom I have known since grade school and with whom I have remained in contact throughout the years.

Typically, we will talk at least once each year, just to catch up. We also work on our high school reunions every five years, which means many more conversations and some meetings. Nevertheless, on one particular day, (for no reason?), I felt the need to call my friend. When he answered, he told me that morning, he was thinking of me and had planned to call.

By the way, this particular friend, Bill Callaghan, has written his own book, called, 'Raise with Praise', which recounts his and his family's lives together, through a spiritual and prayerful journey. Bill tells of his own experiences with God, which includes protection from his own angel (as seen in a shadow in a family picture).

Another event comes to mind, with regards to "chance" meetings and encounters. Long ago, while living in Chicago, my sister Lisa and I made plans to visit. She was coming from Minneapolis, via Milwaukee, and somehow we were going to find each other on the subway train. At the time, Lisa and I were experiencing many similar clairvoyant moments.

I do not recall all the particulars of the visit,

but I do know we had talked ahead of time about where we would meet and how she would find my apartment. Remember, in those days, we did not have cell phones to assist with these matters.

What I do recall is that Lisa was going to be late and I wasn't sure how we would find each other. For some reason, I decided to walk a few blocks to the subway and walked down into the station. As I entered, Lisa walked off the train and we made immediate contact.

On another occasion, I was on a solo kayak trip at one point several years ago. It was a beautiful day and I decided to stop paddling, while in the middle of a wide river. I sat back and enjoyed the sun and the eagles flying overhead. It was one of those moments when you can appreciate God's presence.

At the same time, I felt strong feelings for

my sister Julie, who lived far away in California. That happened quite a bit with the two of us during that period. The next day, we talked and she asked me about eagles and whether I had experienced the pleasure. She told me she had prayed and sent me a message.

On two separate occasions, my great uncle and great aunt died. One was 104 and one was 108 years old. They were both great people, with lots of stories and so much life to share. I saw them on a regular basis, in particular when they were older.

The day that both of them died, I felt them passing into the next world. This was confirmed the day following each of their deaths, when I received a call from my Dad's cousin, informing me of the details. Each time, I asked when they had passed the previous day, and she confirmed it was the precise time I felt their exit from our world.

In the movie, 'Signs', Mel Gibson is a former minister, who has given up his faith, after his wife is lost in a tragic automobile accident. There are aliens who have visited their home and town (and the whole world), leaving Mel Gibson (with his 2 kids) and his brother (played by Joaquin Phoenix), to discuss their fate and chance for survival.

Mel Gibson is resigned to the fact that we are "alone" and that life is just full of a bunch of coincidences. It is not until the end of the movie, when he realizes something spoken by his wife when they last conversed, is not a coincidence at all, but rather a sign (signal, if you will).

A bit earlier in the film, Mel Gibson tells Joaquin Phoenix (Merle in the movie) that his wife uttered, "Tell Merle to swing away". He dismissed this as the crazy signals your brain sends, when near death. As a note, Merle was a minor league baseball player, who set the record for longest home runs. His bat is hung in the living room of the house.

Near the end of the film, an alien has grabbed Mel Gibson's son in the living room and is ready to poison him with lethal gas. At this very moment, the memory of his wife's last words, leads Mel Gibson to say, "Swing away Merle". Joaquin grabs the bat off the wall and pummels the alien guest into submission.

In the very next scene, Mel Gibson is holding his son outside the home. The son is asthmatic and is not responding. After giving his son an injection, Mel Gibson begins to pray and talk to the Lord. He reasons that his son could not be poisoned, since his airway would have been blocked, when the alien injected the lethal gas.

In other words, this is what God had planned and it was true. That is, he had asthma for a reason and his wife uttered those words for a reason. God knew what was coming. The child lives! In the next scene, Mel Gibson is seen putting on his priestly clothes as has decided to return to his ministry, a more humble and satisfied man.

Coincidences or not, many things happen in our lives and universe, which at times, are difficult to explain. However, once you submit to the Lord and begin to believe all is possible, you will be overcome with peace and understanding.

chapter seven:

Constants in our world

We have all had friends and acquaintances throughout our lives, who seem to be there for many reasons. Some stay with you forever, while others drift in and out of our lives, with no apparent agenda. So, too, you may meet strangers, who for some reason, appear to be more than a passing visitor.

Many years ago, my wife and I were engaged and not yet married. As with most couples, we were having some issues and things were not going well at that particular point. It was winter and we were on our way back from somewhere, when we decided to stop and eat at one of our favorite breakfast locations.

There were not many people in the restaurant at the time. I can't recall what time of day it was, but maybe early afternoon? Nevertheless, we sat down at a table and within minutes, a man sat down next to us and we began talking. Keep in mind, there were lots of other available seats in the restaurant, yet he chose one next to us. He was dressed very casual, in sweatpants and tee shirt.

The conversation flowed easily, as he told us about his life and adventures. He asked us questions and somehow he knew about our backgrounds, by his knowledge of our education, families and employment. Looking back, this reminds me of Clarence Oddbody (Angel, Second

Class), from the movie, "It's a Wonderful Life", after he had saved George Bailey.

Needless to say, my wife and I were amazed with how this discussion flowed, yet we didn't realize the full implication, until after we had left the restaurant. During our conversation, the man talked about religion and faith. He talked about his own background, as a Jew. I noticed his eyes. They were blue, deep, and clear as the ocean!

Upon getting ready to leave, the man departed before us, but it seemed in an instant he was gone. We didn't think to ask anyone in the restaurant about the man, or their account of our meeting. However, once we were outside, we noticed there were no footprints in the snow! We thought about all this and realized he must have been an angel, sent to provide us a message about love, faith and commitment.

This same story is also played out in the Christmas shows of the TranSiberian Orchestra (TSO), each and every Holiday Season, for many years. The story and song are told in amazing fashion, as an angel is sent from Heaven, to find the meaning of Christmas.

This angel plays a role in reuniting a young child with her father, whom she has not seen for years. Their relationship had fallen apart at one point (as many do). After the angel intervenes in the life of this child (as well as a bar full of lonely patrons), they all notice no footprints are left in the snow. They all come to the financial aid of the daughter and she is reunited with her father. You will have to see the show or listen to the song for the rest.

Many stories and books have been written about angels and 'spirit guides'. They pass through our world and are present in many forms. I remember reading about strangers who appear in the middle of an emergency or crises, yet no one knows where they came from, nor where they went. They are with us to guide us through our lives – same as our family and friends.

Since I am now 60 years old, I have had many life experiences and acquaintances. Some have been good, while others bad. Yet, through it all, I can now look back and see that certain people have been placed in my life, to guide me towards my goals and ultimate salvation with God.

Many years ago, I was attending an off campus program in Chicago, while attending Ripon College in Wisconsin. This program was named, 'Urban Studies' and designed to immerse the students in city life, with knowledge of politics, social science, psychology, education, etc.

All of us students were assigned to a neighborhood 'precept', which typically included 4-5 apartments, located in several areas of the city. We shared an apartment with students from other Midwest colleges and were assigned a faculty/staff leader. Throughout the semester, we met with this leader to discuss any and all issues, or just to have fun.

At this point in my life, I was 21 years old and I had not spoken to my father in many years. After my parents divorced, things did not go well and I was on my search for life's meaning, as well as role models. As it happened, I became close with the faculty leader and at the end of the program, realized he symbolized a 'father figure' to me.

The reason I tell this story is because I know this was no accident, that this man was placed in my life at the time. Prior to joining this program,

I had planned to travel to Costa Rica for the semester, but had not been able to save enough money during the summer, to pay for that program.

Upon returning to the Ripon campus in the fall to register, I was very disappointed and depressed about the fact that I was going nowhere. When my adviser saw me on campus, he was surprised to see me and asked if I would like to go to Chicago instead. I jumped at the chance and the rest is history.

That experience was one of the best of my life and changed me dramatically, for the better. Had things worked out for Costa Rica, or had I chosen to enroll for regular classes at Ripon that year, nothing would have happened. Instead, this opportunity was provided by God and this time, I chose wisely.

chapter eight:

Real Friends

So too, we choose our friends and acquaintances for many reasons. We may not know it at the time, but some will be temporary, while others last a lifetime. The temporary relationships are always difficult, whether it is several months, or many years. We come together for a reason and then we part. It is never easy.

I have had several friends throughout my life and at this time, am lucky to have at least 4-5, who I know I can count on forever. In the past, I had many more, but they have moved on and life goes on. Looking back, I can see all of them were placed in my life for a reason.

My friend Vince and I were friends since high school, but spent a lot of time together, after my divorce and leading up to my second marriage. We camped, biked, and attended Brewer and Packer games. We had so much fun and these memories will last a lifetime.

During this period in my life, I was not in a good place. I did not feel good about who I was, nor where I was going, in particular with women. Vince (and his wife Renee as well) sacrificed a lot during this period, by spending time with me and leading me to my wife Ellie.

Without them, this marriage would not have occurred. He was my best man.

However, once we were married, bought our home and had our first daughter, we did not see as much of Vince, Renee and their kids. They became busy with their lives and us, with ours. There was nothing wrong with that. Sometimes, it is the way life goes.

I have come to realize, however, that they were placed in my life during that period, because God sent them to me. I was a mess and they were only one of the many, whom I was blessed with, as true friends. We still communicate periodically and I know they still care, but I miss them both every day of my life. The same goes for two other friends, who, coincidentally, came into my life during the same period.

Before I divorced from my first wife, we lived in an apartment complex, where I met Dave and Greg. We spent a lot of time together and shared many good times. I can't tell you how many conversations we had about women, marriage and choosing the right person. After Greg had split up with his girlfriend and I with my first wife, he and I ended up moving to another apartment complex.

Shortly thereafter, I met my future wife Ellie, yet I was uncertain whether I wanted to get serious. Keep in mind I had already messed up enough of my life prior to that relationship, so wasn't so sure I wanted to 'jump right in'. Too bad for Ellie, of course, since my uncertain signals made it difficult for her to know what I was thinking.

Nevertheless, we of course, were married and my two friends Dave and Greg were in the wedding. However, again, as with my best man Vince, once we progressed in our lives and they in theirs, we lost touch and nowadays, infrequently cross paths.

The lesson in all this is that you never know

what awaits you at times, and usually, do not understand the reason(s), until much later. All these people were placed in my life by God, to help me through a very difficult time in my life. Ultimately, this process led, not only to my marriage, but my awakening, as a child of God.

chapter nine:

Awakenings

It was 1994 and I was 35 years old. I had recently divorced from my first wife and was living on my own in an apartment. Nearby was a Catholic church, built in 1868. It was an old church, built in the style of the day – small, quaint, and full of character.

At this point in my life, I felt the urge to return to the Church. I began attending and not long after, my future wife Ellie accompanied me to service on a periodic basis. As you may recall, I was not absolutely certain where our relationship was headed and coincidentally, I felt the same about my faith and the Catholic Church.

As if by design, however, God had already made up his mind. It just took another beating on the head to realize what was happening. As you know, I had always made the wrong choices when God came calling. In the past, I had always dated needy women and felt I would be able to meet those needs and make them happy. I know – lots of co-dependence here.

Either way, what is interesting is that I never looked for reasons not to date (or marry in one case) these women. Instead, I just jumped right in with the same old pattern, became disillusioned and depressed, and ended in the same place.

This scenario reminds me of George Constanza in the Seinfeld show, who- after always making wrong choices and ending up in trouble- decides to 'do the opposite'. He reasoned - if I do the opposite of what I always do, then my life will be right. That does seem to work at times, by the way.

Prior to meeting Ellie for the first time, I decided that I would try the opposite, with my approach. Rather than try to impress her with my good looks and witty charm (yeah, right, she would say), I decided to lay it all on the line and wait for the result. As George figured, "What do I have to lose?"

I told her my age (I am 12 years older than her) and that I was divorced, with no children (truth). I told her I had a bad back and that sometimes, I need to rest and get related treatment. I mentioned other things I can't recall and the funny thing was - she was most interested in whether I had a job, a functioning automobile, a driver's license, and did not live with my parents.

I guess it helps that Ellie had lower expectations, because I could certainly meet those at the time. As our relationship progressed, in spite of my fighting it, I found that maybe this is where I belonged. Why was it though, that I found someone pretty, attractive, honest, and genuine, yet kept looking for reasons not to commit to the relationship?

Everyone liked Ellie and she had so many qualities that I admire. In addition, she had a fun family and a large group of friends, who always made me feel welcome. I am grateful for all of the amazing experiences I have had, as a result of our relationship. There was no reason not to commit.

One day, I was sitting in my car and I felt 'tingles' in my body and simultaneously, felt the voice of God instructing me to marry Ellie. I had never felt anything so strong in my life, but I guess God had to knock real hard this time, since I did not open the door in the past.

chapter ten:

Small Sacraments

I finally listened to God, Ellie and I became engaged and we were then married in the same church I began attending a few years earlier. During the period between the engagement and marriage, we met our priest at the time, Father Charlie, to discuss issues and plans for the wedding (God rest his soul).

We talked about God and I mentioned the 'tingles'. He advised us those were considered small 's's', or sacraments – a message from God. We mentioned the chance meeting with our angel and he seemed to agree the messenger was sent to bring us together.

I relate all of this now, because my life really was going nowhere, before I met and married Ellie. As far as I am concerned, she is an angel herself. No one should have to tolerate me and my ways for all these years. But this was just the beginning of many awakenings and spiritual experiences.

My father died less than a year after we were married. My daughter Jayme was born the following year. Within 2 years' time, one of my best friends, Bob recovered from Hodgekins Lymphoma, only to pass away suddenly, not long after our daughter Payton was buried. During the same period, another good friend from high school died as well.

During and after all of these events, Ellie and I

had many dreams, visions and visits, in particular with my dad and Bob. My dad's second wife stayed with us for a couple days, prior to his funeral. She slept in the other bedroom at our apartment. After the first morning, Ellie woke up and told me she had a 'visit' from my dad, while she slept.

Now, this 'visit' could be interpreted in a number of ways. However, many books have been written and stories related, which discuss the 'spirit' world and connections to the soul. This typically arrives in the form of a dream. My understanding is that your soul and others are able to communicate, by means of these visits, or dreams.

In this case, my dad was visiting with Ellie. She told me he was walking behind a glass door or window and waving at her. He was dressed as always, in his old clothes, wearing his favorite yellow sweater. She said he wasn't talking, but appeared to be happy and content. When Ellie began to tell us of the 'visit', my stepmom said she had the same dream!

Sorry folks, this is not a coincidence. This was my dad, making his presence known (through God, mind you), while sending a message to my wife and his wife, that he was fine. Keep in mind as well my story related previously, about my dad's presence in the car, when I had my back pain.

After my friend Bob passed away, Ellie and I had many visits from our friend. One of hers involved a conversation about how he was doing at the time. Bob told Ellie he was fine and that his ankle no longer hurt, but that he was burned. This left her confused. We reasoned that perhaps Bob's soul had not fully left his body at the time of cremation and that this burn was a reminder?

However, as these things happen, not even a week later, Ellie happened to run into Bob's wife Mary at the Lombardi Run for Cancer, which was an annual event for many years. In the past year, Ellie had run in Bob's honor. When she told Mary of the dream, she said his left ankle always hurt, from standing all day as a chef.

Mary continued and related to Ellie that she had Bob cremated, since it was less expensive than a burial. Apparently, Bob and Mary had talked about this in the past and he was against this method. These were two things we were unaware of, prior to the dream and talking to Mary.

By the way, Ellie's dream (or visit) with Bob took place on a beautiful warm beach by a large government like building with huge pillars and large steps, like a courthouse. Bob said this is where all his meetings took place. To me, this sounds like the 'hall of souls'?

Another time, I had a long visit with Bob and we were walking and talking in a beautiful area, with an outdoor pool, under a glass dome cover. The best thing about this visit (and others I have had) was that you talk and hear, without speaking and listening.

This phenomenon (or ability) is immortalized in the Song, Sounds of Silence, by Simon and Garfunkel. To paraphrase, the lyrics were as follows -'People talking without speaking, people hearing without listening'. It is a form of communication and understanding, which can come only from God.

Bob told me he was doing well and asked how I was doing? I then asked if we could go somewhere, though I can't recall the exact destination. He said we could do that and I asked how we would get there. He kind of shrugged his shoulders and motioned to his wings. Silly me, I was thinking.

chapter eleven:

Spiritual Travel

How many of you have had dreams where you are flying? I do remember this happened to me a lot when I was younger. I never gave much thought to it, but always enjoyed the experience. It wasn't until this point in my life, however, that these travels became more frequent.

Referring back to the soul and the ability to show up in dreams or visits, the flying adventure is a fairly common occurrence. Most people dismiss it, however, as a dream, rather than an opportunity to make contact with the 'spirit' world.

Based upon my experiences and what I have read, those who are not open to, or who dismiss these 'visits' or dreams, will not remember these events. Meanwhile, those who embrace the experience, open themselves up to more opportunities.

My sister Kathy was married to a man several years back, who was undergoing surgery, for a liver transplant. I had talked to both of them on the day prior to the surgery and wished them well, before praying throughout the day and night. That night, I had a 'visit' with this man and we parted with the understanding that surgery was successful and peace was granted.

I spoke to him a couple days later and asked if he had any strange dreams, while under anesthesia or during recovery. I always ask others in this context, so I do not scare them off. He told me no, though I mentioned the specifics of our contact and maybe it gave him something to think about?

Not long after, my sister called and left me a message, telling me she had to talk to me about something. By the way, I had visited a friend of mine earlier that day, who had always been involved in spiritual readings and related activities. She told me that one of my sisters would be calling that night, to share some news with me. That turned out to be true.

Kathy was very excited when I called her. She told me she had a 'flying' dream for the first time and wondered, "What was that?" I can't recall all the details, but she talked about how free and light she felt on this journey. As she had always been skeptical about these kinds of things, I reminded her to remain open to the possibilities.

chapter twelve:

The non-believers

Can you imagine what Jesus went through during his short life time? No matter where he went, people followed, while others questioned and mocked him. His reward for teaching goodness and peace was a hanging on the cross! Fortunately, we are able to use this as a symbol for Jesus' sacrifice for mankind.

What Jesus (and many others) have endured throughout the years, speaks to the hesitancy involved, when relating faith and truth to others. Let's face it – some people are just mean their whole lives and will do anything to maintain that attitude. Others are just afraid to consider the possibilities.

My sister Julie and I have experienced a number of special events throughout the years, whether feelings, visits or extraordinary coincidences. However, whenever we mentioned these events to family members, we were either dismissed or mocked. This did not stop either of us from relating these happenings, though we came to expect the usual response.

Eventually, however, my brother Joe asked me about these occurrences, at a time in his life when he was examining his place in the world. Also, as I related above, my sister Kathy had her 'flying' experience, which opened her mind and soul to the possibilities.

Throughout the past several years, Ellie and

I have also noticed many pictures, which reveal glowing 'orbs' in the midst of the people in the pictures. One of the first times she noticed was in a picture of my sister Kathy, during a visit with my stepmom.

Kathy had not visited with Vicki in a long time. This took place after my dad had passed away and of course, there were many photos. In one picture with just the two of them, there was a bright 'orb' hovering right between them. There was my Dad.

On another occasion, I visited my brother Joe and we were together on Father's Day, after my dad had passed away. Again, good pictures were taken and sure enough, there was another glowing 'orb'. My dad sure appeared to be busy during this period.

There have been many other occasions where

we have noticed these 'orbs', with all of them typically showing up during special events. One of these included Matthew's First Communion and another included Ellie's grandmother's funeral. More recently, at my daughter's graduation party, there were at least two dozen in several different pictures, at twilight in our back yard.

I talk about these issues, because there are many who dismiss these as lights or reflections. However, again, could it be coincidence that God and his followers are choosing these particular close family events, to reveal He (and they) are with us? We need to think again and open ourselves to the possibility.

Throughout His entire life, Jesus faced doubters and non-believers. No one believed it when He changed water to wine. Nobody believed He made a blind man see. No one considered it possible that He brought Lazarus back to life. He had His followers, but He had more haters.

Why is it that we believe only what we can see? What is faith about anyways? We love our children, but how can you prove that? There is no scientific evidence. We believe that a million dollars exists, yet I'm guessing that no one has ever seen a million dollars?

Then why is it so difficult to believe that Jesus, or God exists, when we witness and experience feelings and events that make it difficult – Not to Believe? I always believed that God (and Jesus) existed, yet I was unaware, how strong the belief would become.

chapter thirteen:

The Warm Embrace

It was 2008 and I was 48 years old. I was married, with two kids. I owned my own company and for the most part, life was good. We lived in a nice home. We had plenty of family and friends and really – there was nothing to complain about.

However, I was not happy and could not figure the reason. I thought it might be the depression that lurks in my family history and I considered whether I had to make some major changes in my life. I then had my 'dream'.

In my dream, I was asking God why life was so

difficult and why I was not happy. It was not a long conversation, but rather a sharing of feelings that I felt at the time. I then experienced magnificent warmth and the immediate presence of my mom.

I figured my mom was comforting me at the time as well, through her own dream or visit. By the way, I asked her the next day about it, but she couldn't remember anything. Either way, as she has been through my entire life, my mom was comforting.

Nonetheless, within moments, I saw and felt brightness and warmth, which I had never experienced. I didn't say anything for a few seconds, while I enjoyed the feeling and then asked, "Who are you?" God did not have to answer, as I instantaneously felt His response. All He said to me was, "Five more years". I woke up crying (or weeping) and related the story to my wife.

A few years earlier, I experienced a similar (though not as strong) presence of God. Our daughter Payton had passed to Heaven in 2002. Our friends Sue and Tim were expecting their second child, a boy they named Adam, though at the time, they did not know the gender of the child until after his birth.

At this time, I was driving on my way to work and there was a light and fluffy snow falling. This was the type with real big and soft flakes. It was a quiet and silent moment on the road. At that instant, I felt the presence of our beautiful daughter Payton and was overcome with tears of sadness.

After going home later that day, I related the story to Ellie and she told me she had experienced the same feeling, while taking a shower that morning. She also said that Payton told her a baby was coming and it was going to be a boy. Soon that same day, we found out that Adam had been born at the same time my wife and I experienced the presence of Payton.

We reasoned that our angel daughter was sent by God, to accompany our friend's new baby to his parents, his home and his sister, Lauren. How could there be any other explanation and how could this be dismissed as a coincidence?

About 4 years later, Ellie was scheduled to present at a local hospital, regarding her story with Payton. As you may recall, this was a very difficult time in our lives, yet since then, Ellie decided to contribute a gift annually to the neonatal unit at the hospital, where this all occurred. It was her way of continuing Payton's spirit and helping other families.

This presentation was to be nothing long, but

rather Ellie sharing her story with physicians, nurses, and related health care practitioners. Just prior to this event, she was on her way into the building when she 'passed out.' Fortunately, it was nothing serious and Ellie recovered, but that is not the story.

Ellie told me when this occurred and before she awoke, she felt the presence of our daughter. However, she told me she questioned as if it was Jayme and actually heard, "Mom, it's Payton". So our little girl who had gone to Heaven, was there again, to watch over and bring comfort to her Mom.

All of these events strengthened our beliefs and resolve, while providing some assurance, that those departed are never gone, but with us every day. But the question remains – what about those 5 years that God mentioned above?

Does this mean I will receive 'complete and total consciousness', on my deathbed, as Bill Murray was told by the Dalai Lama (Caddyshack movie)? Or, did it mean that I only have to wait another 5 years, before I can relax and enjoy the Lord's true salvation in my life on this earth?

chapter fourteen:

The Vision Becomes Clear

Not long after the warm embrace, I visited with the friend I referred to earlier. She was actually an acquaintance, but I knew her from several prior social outings. Throughout her life, she had been involved on a regular basis with spiritual counseling and teaching activities.

I had always been interested in the human soul, dream interpretations, philosophy, Native American literature and the "meaning of life". I sensed at this point this would be a good opportunity to spend some time talking to her about these dreams and visits I was having, while trying to shed some light on the meaning.

I had always thought about doing this and for some reason, felt this was the right time. She knew nothing of me, but my name and my connection to our other friend. We decided to meet in her home in a casual setting and just let nature takes its' course.

I really did not know what to expect, but went into the meeting with an open mind. Her house was tastefully decorated and she had a small room in the basement, which was real comfortable. Upon entering her home, she simply greeted me, and then asked me to take a seat downstairs, while she remained upstairs, to jot down some notes.

Once she came down to sit with me, I let her do the talking at first, since, although I believed she was not a fake, I wanted to make sure she knew nothing about me. By the way, she did not steal my wallet, nor could she have had other information, as even my google information was limited (in particular at that time).

One of the first things mentioned was that I had a lot on my mind at the time. She said that I was a non-conformist and that I had a "different way of thinking". She said that I grew up fast and that I feel impatient with process. She said I don't really fit in with any country or society.

I was beginning to feel vulnerable, as she was so accurately describing my past and my innermost feelings. What she said next was the clincher though. It was as if she reached in my soul, grabbed it and was able to hold it in front, while she proclaimed, "YOU ARE BEING TORTURED!"

This woman then proceeded with her impressions and told me that it was as if my spirit had died and that it was a struggle to get up each morning. She said that I felt misplaced and that it could not be another 7 years of this type of pain and suffering. How did she know this was exactly how I felt at the time?

More important, how did she come up with the 7 year figure, as that was exactly how many years it had been, since I began my business. Since then, I expected my whole life would fall into place, so that I could live happily ever after? However, during the entire period since 2002, I had been struggling mightily with what to do for the rest of my life.

At this point, I began crying, since she had been able to zero in on my entire problem. That is, my soul and my spirit were dead and thirsty.

In spite of many blessings and good health, I felt empty and wanting. I had no idea what to do and no plan to rid myself of this feeling.

Next, we talked about more mundane and interesting things, yet she still hit the mark. She told me that I "struggle" a lot during the day and that I am "out of focus", in particular when I am on the road driving. In fact, she said she doesn't like me driving at all.

As additional background, aside from the major accident I had many years ago (the rollover), I have been involved in 4 other accidents, which resulted in damage (some extensive) to my car(s). Also, I have been involved in several other incidents, which would be considered close calls.

Fortunately, I have had no accidents or near accidents with the kids in the car and I have to say, I am much more careful, since beginning to care for a family in 2000. However, there have been many occasions when I "lose focus", as described by this woman.

At one point during the conversation, this woman was describing some of her thoughts, by telling me she wondered, "Did he stop at the sign?" I immediately began to think of all the times when I might have done just that. In other words, driven right through a red light, or just done something stupid at an intersection.

As we continued, this woman began talking about how I prefer to be 'on water', which has always been the case. Nothing relaxes me better than jumping in a lake, river or pool, or possibly, kayaking, or hiking, so long as I am by the water. Within the same context, she affirmed my need to retreat, seek pilgrimage and connect with nature.

At this point, it was hard not to believe in the

accuracy of this woman's abilities. She proceeded by accurately describing my daughter Jayme's unique and creative nature, complete with combative emotions, but also her special talents and beauty, which make her so special. She talked about my son Matthew and his beautiful soul (and nature), as if she had spent intimate time in his company.

As we continued, this woman talked about my dad, in the context of other issues. She accurately described how he was 'calmer', in comparison to most in our family. She also talked about my deceased good friend Bob, by reporting that he did not like sadness and that he was 'light, fun, and zany'. I could not agree more.

All of these impressions and readings were based solely upon her personal insight and abilities, yet supported by factual events and personal feelings experienced throughout my life. Also, she later showed me her notes (written before we met), which correctly identified the many issues we had discussed.

I was beginning to understand more about who I was and why I felt certain things during this time - yet the clincher was not yet revealed.

chapter fifteen:

The Knockout Punch

During the course of my consultation and conversation with this woman, many things became clear. However, it wasn't until she touched upon a very sensitive subject, when I truly began to believe, while at the same time, felt the dark shadow begin to lift from my heart and soul.

As I have already reported in previous chapters, I have had many experiences, dreams, and related events occur in my life. I faced these with doubt initially, but soon began to embrace these as part of my special relationship with God.

At one point, this woman expressed her belief that my special relationship with God and Jesus was just that. She suggested I was one of those people who have experiences and insights, which bring people closer to God, so long as they pay attention and apply those insights. She also postulated that much of my anguish and sadness was derived from my personal feelings about Jesus and the disciples.

Little did she know (which I explained to her at this point), that I indeed had always felt sad and wanting, in particular during the Easter season, but also any time at Church or elsewhere, when the Jesus stories are related. Many times, I have cried listening to gospels about the pain and suffering He endured, throughout His life.

At the same time, I have always been sensitive to the nature of society and behavior of humans, when it comes to personal interaction, wars, television, media, etc. This woman confirmed this as well, when she mentioned I am unable to watch anything on television, which speaks or portrays violence, mistreatment, and inhumanity.

During our meeting, this woman told me that, "My existence has nothing to do with my wife and kids". She did not say that or mean that in a derogatory manner, but rather as a means to identify my struggle and my need to pursue a higher goal. In fact, she actually confirmed that my wife and kids were doing fine, by describing their many deeds and blessings.

Near the end of our meeting, this woman then confirmed one of my beliefs that I have held for many years, yet did not officially incorporate into my daily existence, in particular with my relationship to God. That is, the "coolest things" that have happened to me, happened on their own schedule. They happened when I least expected it, yet always when I needed it most.

chapter sixteen:

It All Comes Together

After that visit, I was able to settle down and relax. All of a sudden, everything made sense to me. Not that I was going to be perfect and never make mistakes again, but at least I now had an understanding of where I had been and where I was going.

Throughout my life, I have felt restless and wanting. That is one reason I have always chosen to hike, kayak, camp or just take a drive. In the past, on a regular basis, it was not unusual for me to escape for a day or two, sleep in my van at a campground, make fires and commune with nature.

Other times, I may need to get away for a few hours, for the same reason. I usually do the same thing, for a momentary feeling of peace. We all need breaks at different times, for one reason or another. Mine, though, seem directly tied to who I was and who I have become.

I truly believe that I have been a follower of Christ for a long time, but just was not aware. Also, I have always felt as though I lead somewhat of a gypsy and/or travelling life. That would explain the restlessness and the need to commune with nature. It would explain as well my need to be near water and enjoy fire. On a funny note, it explains why I have always worn bandanas, once had an earring and still enjoy jewelry.

I have heard, or read somewhere, about

studies which suggest we are all born with certain traits or memories and that we live our lives, while carrying certain experiences from our ancestors. Think about how we all have such traits from our mothers, fathers, grandmas, grandpas, uncles and aunts.

Why then, would it be so difficult to accept that we translate those traits and lives, as we adapt to our daily life? For the same reasons I cannot bear to hear or visualize the treatment of Jesus, I am unable to tolerate similar behavior and tendencies in my current life.

If I presume I lead more of a gypsy life, it explains why the spiritual adviser told me I prefer bartering, rather than a money exchange system. It also explains why to this day, I am not so concerned about money to purchase material goods or items, but rather as a means to provide the freedom and flexible life that I cherish.

Of course, all of this is well and good, yet there is still the need to carry on as a human, father, husband, brother, uncle, friend, or child of God. If I truly want to succeed in this capacity, what would be my next move?

chapter seventeen:

The Meaning

One of the basic understandings of Native Americans is that "The Great Spirit" has given us this life and treasures, as a gift. It is our job to cherish these gifts with love and respect. For some reason, of course, our white ancestors could not understand their "Great Spirit", as this entity did not match theirs in form, shape, or history.

However, in the Ten Commandments and teachings of Christ, we are taught to treat others, as we would like to be treated. We should speak the truth, hold fast to our bargains, not covet another's wife, and love thy neighbor. The same concepts are repeated again and again. At the same time, "The Great Spirit" sees and hears everything.

In my mind, the Native Americans are the ones who got it right. They were in awe of each new day. They hunted only for what they needed – and nothing more. They gave thanks for their gifts and they respected Mother Earth. They respected their elders. Each night, they gave thanks and waited for a new day. What was their reward for this way of life?

No matter your age, gender, religion, or beliefs, we all live in this world together and struggle to find our way. We are given gifts from God before we begin our lives and it is His intention that we discover those gifts and share them with others.

It us up to each of us to open our hearts and souls, to become close to God.

I have learned all of this throughout my life and had all of these experiences. I always wondered about what was next and what else should I be doing. I never thought that I should just let Christ take over and lead me in His direction, though that become much easier, once I embraced the meaning.

chapter eighteen:

The Journey Home

A long time ago, I was born into this world, with little knowledge of what was ahead. Had I been wiser in my earlier years, I could have saved myself and others several painful and needless experiences. Fortunately, as our God is always good, He provides you multiple opportunities for enlightenment and salvation. He forgives you your sins, and always provides you with another chance.

Whether your past or your current life activities and contributions play a bigger role, no one can say for sure. However, I know now that my life is the result of many events, interactions and actions. Each one leads to the next and my choices have a direct effect on who I become.

In the movie, 'Field of Dreams', starring Kevin Costner, there is a scene when he meets Terrance Mann (played by James Earl Jones). Terrance was a popular writer during the 1960's, who spoke and wrote of love and peace as his message, rather than hate and war.

Prior to this meeting, Kevin Costner had a dream (or vision), in which he meets Mr. Mann and actually sits with him at Fenway Park, to watch the Red Sox play a baseball game. He tells his wife of the dream the following morning and suggests he needs to go to Boston (from Iowa), to find Mr. Mann.

During this period, Kevin and his wife are

struggling financially, since they have torn up many acres of their cornfield to build a ballpark. He was encouraged to do this first by a voice (God and his soul?) and then by other visitors during the movie.

As Kevin relates his dream and the need to leave, his wife asks details about Fenway and where he was sitting, by proclaiming she had the same dream. To make a long story short, Kevin leaves for Boston, finds Mr. Mann, and attempts to convince him he needs to go to the game, since he expects something will happen.

Of course, this is met by disbelief by Mr. Mann, as he has long departed from the public eye and chooses now to live inconspicuously, while writing and producing videos about ways for children to peacefully resolve their differences. In other words, he does not believe Kevin and this leads to various attempts by Mr. Costner, to relay his message.

At one point, Kevin relates, "There comes a time when the cosmic tumblers click into place, to show you what is possible." Terrance Mann rebuffs him by exclaiming, "You're from the 60's" and "There's no place for you."

After the door is shut, after almost getting beat up, Kevin Costner is finally given a chance, when Mr. Mann relents and goes along with the plan. The rest of that story is history, as they say. However, the point is – had Kevin Costner not taken that first step forward, nothing would have happened.

Don't let this be your fate as well. Look for the signs - listen to your soul, your conscience and God. Let Him lead the way and you will not be disappointed. In fact, your life will become simpler each day, as you follow the path to your own salvation. Take one step forward, and walk with God.

EPILOGUE:

Ironically, it had been almost 5 years in 2013, since my dream (or vision) with God, as well as my visit with the spiritual acquaintance. During those years, I set out to accomplish several tasks, some which I completed and others, still in the works. One of those included my decision to join a Christian Church and volunteer.

This decision was not easy, since we had been very active in our Catholic Church. I served as a trustee at one point. My wife taught religious education. We both served as marriage counselors for those planning to wed in the church.

By this time, though, my kids were getting older (about 13 and 8) and they (like me), were no longer that interested in continuing to participate. I suggested we attend the Christian Church on a regular basis, though my wife was a bit reticent. However, within a short period of time, we all decided to attend each week.

Since that time, we have enjoyed the pastors and the work of this Christian Church and more importantly, the kids mostly looked forward to attending. In fact, my daughter decided on her own to be baptized again (total immersion) and many times, attended on her own or with friends. As many of you know, if you can get a teenager to Church, that is a great step.

Aside from that entire change, the most important event that occurred in 2013, was that I felt compelled to write this book. Nothing would get in my way! Some of you might think that I waited for just this moment, since I knew my five years was up.

However, much to the contrary, I didn't realize until I began this process again and then listened once more to my notes and a recording of my spiritual reading, that the time was here. As reported above, the coolest things happen to me, when they happen and when least expected.

It is now 2019 and six years since that time. Many other events and life changes have come along, including my diagnosis of non-Hodgekins Lymphoma shortly after Christmas 2016. Without going into detail, that has become my biggest challenge, though God has blessed us here as well.

Without any type of treatment or therapy, I have been able to stabilize (and possibly regress) the progressive nature of this disease. I have used natural remedies, the support of many family and friends, and most of all, my savior, Jesus Christ.

I can truly say that I am in a much better place, compared to the many times in my life, when I was lost. I have been married to my wife 21 years now and it has not always been easy, but we have shared so many good things. My kids are doing very well and I am still working with my business.

More importantly, I have found new peace and understanding, along with patience, while I continue my efforts to please God and fulfill His desire for my mission on earth. It is not all clear, yet the more I open my soul, the easier my life becomes. I believe I finally completed this book, because He felt it was time.

ACKNOWLEDGEMENTS:

First and foremost, I thank God and his Son Jesus Christ for the opportunity to live and learn through the Holy Spirit and contribute to His mission for me on earth.

I thank my Mom for bringing me into this world and her comfort and support throughout all her years.

I thank my wife Ellie for her love and patience and staying by my side, through the good and the bad.

I thank my kids, Jayme and Matthew, for the

opportunity to father and lead them through this life and their own journeys.

I thank my daughter Payton, who has been an inspiration and beautiful spirit, leading us all closer to God.

I thank my siblings and all my family and friends (past and present), who have been with me the whole way. Without you, my life would not be complete.

About the Author

He graduated with a Bachelor's degree in Sociology/ Anthropology and a Master's degree in Education. He worked for several years as a counselor and administrator in colleges and universities, as well as in a career consultant capacity with his own business, assisting individuals and groups with personal and professional goals. He served many years as a volunteer in education and church settings. His personal experiences have included many moments of joy, grief, uncertainty, and love, leading him to a special relationship with God.